# DON'T SHAKE THE SPOON

## A Journal of South Florida

## Prison Writing

## Vol. 1

Edited by

Ben Bogart

**DON'T SHAKE THE SPOON**
A JOURNAL OF SOUTH FLORIDA PRISON WRITING
VOL. 1,
August, 2018


*Editor: Ben Bogart*
*Co-editor: Kim McGrath-Moreira*
*Managing Editors:  Enzu Castellanos, Kate Cruz*
*Production Intern: Mahitha Devi Kunamneni*
*Interns: Galia Bernat, Elizabeth Davis, Graham Watkins*
*Advisory Board: Enzu Castellanos, Kathie Klarreich, Josh Schriftman*
*Cover photo: Luis Fernando Salazar*
*Publisher: Exchange for Change, Kathie Klarreich, Director*

**EXCHANGE**

**FOR CHANGE**

**Writing that Transforms**

www.exchange-for-change.org

2103 Coral Way, 2nd Floor
Miami, FL 33145

(305) 771-3241

# Table of Contents

**Don't Shake the Spoon**  by Eduardo Martinez

Sitting in these hot, concrete coffins, we burn more calories than we consume.  We are allotted the minimal amount of proteins and carbohydrates to carry us to the next meal.  God forbid you do pushups. There goes the biscuit from our already meager trays. *And that's if they didn't shake the spoon.*

Three meals a day:  the first one usually yawning into 5 AM, the last meal nipping at the heels of 5 PM.  Chow halls are designed by the same evil genius, because they're all structured to prevent us from peeping behind the oven, inside the chow pot, and from losing our appetites.

What does it *taste* like?  It tastes like "chow"—whatever the hell that means—and if you don't like it, pride is just as edible.  Nevertheless, "chow" is food. *Sometimes* it's even hot food, and for most individuals, it's all they have.  So regardless of the weather, the lines remain long with traffic jam rage, cookies are traded for experimental "meat" patties, and Chicken Tuesday is "Bardyard Pimp" night.  Plastic sporks, oily cups, greasy trays that refuse to relinquish the residue of the previous meal, flies, stains . . . napkins? *What napkins?*

Whatever the flavor, it doesn't matter.  There's nothing we can do about it. Besides, we're all there for one purpose: *we're*

1

*hungry*. And hunger gets ugly. Especially when appetites come with attitudes provoked by circumstances and guards.

The finish line: A Jack-O'-Lantern's missing tooth; a rectangular shape; a black eye on a waffle bland wall, where an inmate's saggy, sweaty, soggy-gloved hand pushes out trays weaker than newborns. Trays that add contractions to the hunger pains.

Still, you accept this tray, hesitant and with multiple choice reactions as you feel the man's eyes behind you roll over your shoulder, followed by the disappointed mumble of, "*Damn*. They shook the spoon."

Some men remain humble and hungry as they ungracefully carry their scraps to their tables. Very few men voice their frustration and famishment by attempting to look through the filthy food flap and hurl insults to the men behind the scenes on the serving line—men who happen to be fellow felons.

Institutionalized, or programmed? A prisoner's paradox. It's either *shake the spoon* on their co-convicts who cling to bread crumbs due to lack of support, budget cuts, and come-ups; or lose a dollar, work a little harder for free, and go to the box for having empathy.

Most often, what's deserved is never given. What's expected is lost. Dropped. Along with hope, family, and love. Even God plays peek-a-boo with our beliefs. Eventually everything vanishes, including us—fading like hard Xs on marked calendars—

2

'til we evaporate with the fumes of ungranted birthday wishes.

In society, shaking the spoon can simply mean you end up ravenous on a very bad day:  using all your spare change (including the change in the console and ashtray), ordering a six-piece *Chicken McNugget*, and speeding off . . . only to reach your destination, dig into your bag and discover a four-piece. *And no Sweet-N'-Sour sauce . . .*

Those are the tiny, mischievous moments; the temporary forevers in life that suck.  We starve for more than just nutrition.  We hunger for attention, forgiveness, respect, redemption.  These pages are the D.O.C.'s dirty dishes: raw, uncut, no rocks, no filter.  Meals of sadness and sunrays, sugar-watered tears and salty, force-fed fears.  We offer you everything we have. Everything you deserve.

Eat society's delicacies, as the stereotypical tune is drowned by the bass of our hearts.  Eat our words, digest our stories. Eat 'til you're *disgusted*, 'til awareness replaces your appetite.  Fill your conscience with everything . . . everything but broken promises.

EAT!  EAT! EAT!

Then feed us changes, but please . . .

*Don't Shake the Spoon . . .*

'Cause we're starving for freedom.

## Editor's Introduction

When we set out to publish a collection of writings to come out of the *Exchange for Change* program, we really only had one firm maxim:  this needed to be as close to our students' original visions of their texts as possible.

What you hold now is our best attempt to do just that, and a number of considerations have been made as we strive to sit you, dear reader, in front of the works that have captivated us for nearly four years now.  One such consideration was approaching the students themselves for a name for their journal—a call which produced a hefty volume of suggestions. Ultimately, both editors and students alike found Eduardo Martinez's *Don't Shake the Spoon*—the explanation of which you've just read—to be the most reflective of our goals for this endeavor.

We wanted to create a theme for this first volume that would center our writers on the notion of transformation that was important to our program, but to leave that theme open-ended enough that they could write what was on their minds.  So our first call went out for works that addressed, simply enough, "change." What is printed here are the works that best fit that rather simple concept, and as you will see, they run the gamut of potential interpretations. I ask you, as you read, to watch not only for what the students themselves say about change (both personal and societal), but for the topics and tones they bring to the table.

One idea that was presented to me early on in my work with *Exchange for Change* was that prisons are like time-capsules—both ideas and materials are slow to filter in from the "outside," and so those who live and work "inside" necessarily reflect a lag of sorts, as the present seeps into a place that stands apart from the progression of time.  I think the works you see here will contradict that notion. The culture of 2018 feels very much alive and well in these pieces, from our collective perceptions of the current political moment to the social acceptances that have marked the last decade. So as you begin to read these selections, please consider not just how "change" is a word commonly used, but how it shapes the very fabric from which our authors choose to work.

On behalf of the editorial staff and the students whose work makes up this volume, we thank you for reading.   If what you see here resonates with you as it does with us, we hope that you will consider supporting *Exchange for Change*, and that you will watch for future volumes of *Don't Shake the Spoon*.

Ben Bogart, Editor

## Dedications

This collection is dedicated to the incarcerated men and women of South Florida, and their brothers and sisters behind bars throughout the world. It is our hope that while their bodies are confined, their souls, like their voices, can know a greater freedom.

It is also personally dedicated to two Exchange for Change students and contributors to this volume who sadly passed away before printing: Luis Aracena and Luis Hernandez.

Luis Aracena was a long-time student of the E4C program, and a friend to all those who worked with him in class. His works "The Show" and "Greater?" show in detail the kind of dedicated student he was—happy to take advantage of the educational opportunities provided to him, but perhaps saddened by the confinement that kept him from sharing a greater good with those on the outside. In response, Luis became an ambassador for our program at Dade Correctional Institution, bringing new students into the fold each semester, and encouraging their development as writers like a dedicated coach. Luis lives on in the work of students who he will not see grow to full capacity, but who will forever remember the kindness and generosity that made him such a wonderful presence.

Luis Hernandez, whose work also graces the pages of this first issue, was the reigning slam poetry champion of Dade C.I.. A student of *Exchange for Change* from the very beginning, Luis most embodies the spirit of our program by working to revise the text of his own life; finding a "second act" in prison that few could manage in the world-at-large. Through the power of his writing and his unwavering spirt, Luis managed to gain freedom for the last months of his life, and in so doing, showed us all the power of the written word to truly *transform*.

Luis Hernandez reminds us of the potential for change within all of us, and best exemplifies the (often misquoted) words of Mahatma Gandhi: "We but mirror the world. All the tendencies present in the outer world are to be found in the world of our body. If we could change ourselves, the tendencies in the world would also change. As a man changes his own nature, so does the attitude of the world change towards him. This is the divine mystery supreme. A wonderful thing it is, and the source of our happiness. We need not wait to see what others do."

# DON'T SHAKE THE SPOON
## A Journal of South Florida
### Prison Writing

## Vol. 1

**Injustice System**  by Kandis Lear

I'm sitting here miles away.

Missing times in your lives that can never be replaced.

Hurting so much so, that these bars feel

like nails drilled into me so slowly. I am numb, because the minutes

that pass seem like years.

I know my pain is like a scratch covered with only a bandage

compared to your sufferings. I say

sorry a million times, but it will never be enough to undo the

damage that is done. I've broken promises

and made mistakes. I've shared my past and misguided you in my

actions by not appropriately achieving

my future goals.

Yet you've shown me unconditional love, loyalty,

understanding and the maturity of being a

woman, a mother, and a friend. These life struggles and time of

bondage have given me a sincere wake-up call that I am an adult, I

have responsibilities. The desires of my future plans, I have taken

the initiative

to seek and research positive directions in achieving my future

goals.

Lusciously,

Kandis Lear

**Poem About Kathie**  by Ramon Grayson


She came to the room to create a bloom.

Ruin, gloom, and doom.

Turn it into a bloom?


One can't use ruin, gloom, and doom

and create a bloom.  All these ingredients,

no matter what I do,

will turn into a bloom.

*Oh, My,* she exclaimed with a sigh.


A flower proceeds from a seed

if you can meet all its required needs.  Add a little care and love

because it's not a weed

and soon it will be there, sharing its beauty

while putting the smell of pretty in the air.  It might

be thinking, *I'd be at home if I was in Kathie's hair*.


Ruin, gloom and doom,

turn them into a bloom?

She came with snakes,

snails, and puppy dog tails.  Are these the things

blooms are made of?  Who needs what part?

Where

does creativity start?

*How do I change a broken life*

*or a broken heart*?

*I'll teach them what I can*, a woman with a pen

and a plan, *work their inner inspiration and make them give*

*a damn. Create your own thoughts,*

*not just what you've been taught.*

*Write them down and I'll fine tune*

*what work you've been doin',*

*and one day you'll see, writing can be*

*as easy as being free.*

Taught us this and taught us that, gave us inspiration

and even a laugh. Through the molding, growing,

Pruning, she's creating a bloom

just to add a little life

to the room.

Ruin, gloom, and doom

that was turned into a bloom.

Though it's not out yet, one day they'll pay me for my text.

As I'm formed, molded, cultivated and separated,

Separated to become the writer created,

to create the great,

to create writing for which no one can wait.


Line after line

shines in her eyes.

Her blooms reign!

**The Sun Set That Day**  by Michael Gonzalez


The sun set that day

When he announced:

"That's it! There's no possible way he's getting out!"

As he squashed

any naïve request for mercy

under the spiteful swings of his gavel,

while gazing

though lenses glazed

with the charges carried.

Never caring to see me for me.

Scoffing at how powerful a slave-master

drugs can be.

But that's only because *he's* never felt the tug,

the need

the false promises and dreams that consume you

until your next fix—

which does everything but.


The sun set that day.

And I had been prepared

for the pronouncement of a long sentence.

But I was taken aback

by the bad grammar.

For there was nothing

to mark the end of it.


I felt the sun set on my life that day.


Am I responsible for a death?

The rushing of the last breath,

The pushing into eternal rest

Of a precious human being?

Sadly, I must answer: True.

But was *that* my evil intent

In my heart;

 the result,

*exactly* what I meant?

FALSE!

A thousand times false!


But overwhelmed with a sense of guilt

I took the so-called deal handed to me;

ignorant if the intricacies

that even people with law degrees

have a hard time grasping.

So now here *I* stand

gasping,

snatching at

every ghost of a chance,

any whisper of an opportunity,

for someone to get to know me

for just three seconds—

and see that me at 33

is not the same me that I was

at nineteen.


The sun set that day, at nineteen,

And I thought it failed to rise in the next.

But I've since learned

that no matter how permeated the skies with despair,

or how thick the clouds of disappointment,

the sun is *still* there

casting its life onto the world.

And so, as long as there's a rhythm in my chest

I will, in HIM, give my best

By shining light

Into every person I encounter

And exhausting myself

In the betterment of others.

Never giving up hope.

Because though the sun sets today

I can count on it rising in the next.


We can always count on the sun rising in the next.

**The Me Who Is Change** by Roderick Richardson

Sometimes I wonder, *who can I be?* I believe the definition of change starts as a seed. Planted through an act of lust, that human kind sometimes mistaken for love. Just like how one moment it may be dark and cloudy, and the next, the sun's brilliance is shining so bright, and the sky is clear and blue.

The me who is change started out living in poverty, loved by two parents, living the American Dream that really wasn't true. Looking back on times when there was joy, it was believing in Santa Claus and thinking that life was full of happiness and joy. Not knowing that there would be many tear-stained years ahead. From crawling on the floor, to the first steps that man takes, change is of the essence. Because the world that we live in is revolving at a frantic pace.

As the world turns, so do life's experiences continue to grow. Innocence replaced by the need for survival, emotional change built upon the way we view our circumstances and situations. Can one person love another so much that they would sacrifice their one and only soul?

Change in me comes with understanding that, yesterday, I will never see again. Will tomorrow come? It's a question that no man has the ability to know.

Change is knowing me, when at one time, I was lost in the mist of wide oceans, blowing on the breeze. Building a foundation with the passage of time, as solid as brick. Which began as sand.

Change is letting the people I know love me, see who the best of me truly can be. Staying focused, compassionate, realistic, and at the same time, enhancing my mind. Sanity is not an option; strength comes from somewhere hidden deep within. It is tears, joy, and laughter dissolved into one, realizing the God of Invisibility is man's only true friend.

Is it hope or faith that keeps me hanging on? Life can sometimes feel like I'm falling off a cliff, but by a thin thread I continue to keep hanging on. The me who is change can see the difference now from day to day. Knowing that no wrong can defeat a right, no matter how men try to justify it. Change and life are not games. The me who is change can see now that, without change, a person can die and still be alive—a walking zombie with no emotional feelings on the inside.

Change is taking our past, moving forward, and putting a smile on our faces, no matter what we have to endure.

Change is about meeting people different from yourself, while putting yourself in their place. Change is hope that we can't see, but somehow know that it's there. Hidden in the mist of darkness, even when we feel that no one cares. Change is looking in the mirror and seeing the same face that you've seen since you were a child, looking older, growing gray, and holding onto "faith" as a man clinging to a lifeboat, knowing that if he lets go, it's the end.

Change is wishing for change, as the days of my life pass me by.

Change is wanting to be a father, son, big brother, uncle, grandfather, cousin to those I love, and I know who love me. "Family." Our personal genetic source that provides a family tree. The me who is change just wants to be the best me that I can be; to wake up from this nightmare called prison, where insanity is reality.

As the blood flows through my veins, I continue to pray for another chance, day after day. Because the me who is change understands now the priceless gift called "liberty." The me who is change started out a mere seed, and now I've developed into a fully-devoted oak tree.

**Ghost**  by Benjamin Ice


Just the other night I remembered her smile

When thunder shook the air and lightening flashed

She said "Let's go dance in the rain for a little while"

I reached out for her hand as the vision passed


I can still see her eyes, grey and warm like my flannel shirt

I can still feel her kiss where her lips lingered

I can still smell the air, so clean like fresh-turned dirt

As I looked again at the letter in my fingers


Here in Arizona I still miss the rain

You know I never meant to cause you any pain

I hope someday you'll come and visit me again

Or at least send me a postcard when you can


It's been so long since I held you in my arms

Your skins so soft and smooth and warm

But when you went away I knew I'd lost my charm

No more your teddy bear, who keeps you safe from harm


The rain turned quiet, only a memory from the past

I dried my eyes, wiped away the tears at last

I thought I should try and call you once or twice

If only heaven had a toll-free number, wouldn't that be nice?

**When Things Outlive Their Usefulness**  by Allington Dante Dottin

When a thing outlives its usefulness, how does one disengage?

What is the manner of discharge: What means of disposal is used?

It is agreed, one and all, they are left by the wayside

Save the few items we tend to hoard

We do this—either in *spite* of their lack of utility, or in ignorance

thereof

When clear-minded, we certainly replace—or abandon, at least—

said item

But what of people? Emotions? Ideas? What of Belief? Of Faith

itself?

Most things we discard—benefits having Been exhausted—without

thought

Automatically . . .

Directions—once we've learned our way . . .

Recipes—once we've learned the dish . . .

Argument-provoking words—once we learn they cause too much

shit . . .

Shoes—once we've worn out the sole . . .

A pet—once it has released its Soul . . .

Plans and Preparations—once we achieve that goal . . .

But what of people?

Do we toss them away, like roses that have Begun to wilt?

Or like a well-worn coat, pass them down to one less fortunate?

And if that old sweater—the one with the Flame

Should again pass your way, You—politely refuse

"No, thank you. I've another. Good to hear your voice, though.

Been so long."

*'Please don't call again,'* pervading your tone . . . Ahhh, outlived

their usefulness

Oh—and what of emotion? When the temper tantrum is ignored

When the parent realizes the child's But Bored

When the last salt water tear track's scored

That face adored, without reward . . . s/he discards it

When self-pity throws a fashion Ball

And not a guest shows up at all

When nary a god answers the call, for intercession

It Begs the question: What of Faith: What of Belief?

When everything seems to go . . . *Not* your way

But still, you hold fast anyway

When, "one day at a time, just get thru today," turns 5,093 old

When you conclude that you're tired of all the rapping

That true Spirituality is devoid of all the trappings

When you Begin to age—spiritually grown—And realize you are *not*

at Home

That you've simply followed all you've *ever* known

So you Begin to Search, to seek, to roam

And while certain overstanding escapes us in youth

While not everything—to us—has concrete 'proof'

The undeniable fact remains . . .

The Highest Religion is *TRUTH*

All they put forth in these tumultuous times

All they dance and sing and chant and rhyme

Is so distorted and misaligned

Worshipping the symbols and the signs . . . the *Blinds*

Instead of the Sublime, the Truths that lay Behind

Control and Blind faith, contrary and inimical to the *Original Design*

This registers in my Heart & Soul, not merely a calculation of the mind

When all I knew, and held to Be true, is nowhere to find

I ask again: *What do you do when a thing outlives its usefulness?*

**The Parallels of Change**  by Francois Richardson


Let's talk about change: A word that has been surfing the airwaves of media, especially social media, very strongly over the past ten years. So, I guess we should start with the man who gave this word its popularity, Mr. Barack Obama.

If I had to make a super hero inspired from the word "change," Obama would be the perfect candidate. Just for the sake of having fun, I'll make him the leader of *The Changeables*.

I would adorn Mr. Change with blue tights. I would have the American flag with the words "Mr. Change" emblazoned on his chest. I would give him an all-red cape. And I would equip him with a belt that turns into a robotic eagle from the tap of a button.

I guess he couldn't be the leader of The Changeables without a team. Joe Biden would be his right-hand man, like Beast is to Professor X. I would make Hillary Clinton and Susan Rice his ass-kicking, karate sisters. And I would make Paul Ryan co-pilot of the team's super-charged plane called "Vortex," a.k.a Air Force One. Plus, Mr. Ryan seems fit for a Robin mask. I could see Marvel Comics licking its chops.

All this actually seems really easy to imagine. But you can't be called "Mr. Change" and be leader of The Changeables without proof of some positive change that you've enacted to better the lives of the American people. So let's put him under the microscope:

According to *CBS News* the recession that Mr. Change inherited is close to being obliterated. The economy has added 13.7 million new jobs over a sixty-nine month streak of job growth. The latest unemployment rate figures dropped to 5% in October 2016. On Obamacare, the Supreme Court ruled in favor (6-3) of upholding a major part of it, allowing the federal government to give out subsidies to its consumers in all states no matter whether they sign up through federal- or state-based exchanges.

Mr. Change's America took the lead on certain issues such as global warming, which got a boost of energy with the COP 21 climate talks in Paris, where a deal was reached to reduce greenhouse gas emissions.

Mr. Change held true to his "unclenched fist" policy with countries the United States has had terrible, if not horrible, relations with for decades: Iran and Cuba. Mr. Change struck a landmark nuclear deal with Iran involving six other world powers. And the American flag was raised at the United States embassy in Cuba for the first time in 54 years.

He signed the Trans Pacific Partnership trade deal involving twelve Pacific Rim countries. He orchestrated an education overhaul with No Child Left Behind, while also pushing for the bipartisan budget deal that avoided the threat of a government shutdown.

He also ended two wars, and didn't start one. He gave the mass incarceration movement a shove in the right direction. In my opinion, there were a lot of positive changes during Obama's two terms in office. Many in the Republican party would take me to task about that last sentence, though.

Their disbelief of the evidence that sits right in their face reminds me of the disbelief that most of society holds about change in prisoners. So maybe it's no wonder that shove wasn't enough.

Change is like everything else in life. There's good and bad to it. So of course when we change, we want to change for the better. For change has been at the epicenter of our universe since the beginning of time. If civilizations don't learn to evolve, they'll most likely become extinct.

So change comes about whether we want it or not, even in prison. The important thing to ask is, is it progressive? Does it help people? And if so, how do we gauge this progression in prisoners? And perhaps most importantly, what can we as a society do to make sure that prisoners are getting the proper help to bring about this positive change in them?

Educate them, sure. But knowing this is only half the battle. Because there's many things that one can do by way of self-education while doing time, but most choose not to do anything. I mean, something as simple as reading a novel every day will take you to new heights.

The D.O.C should consider what one of my classmates suggested during one of our class's furious "Ms. K Forums": making education compulsory for all prisoners. If you tie it in to gain time, most prisoners' motivation will peak through the roof.

Why make it compulsory? I'll use our movement (Exchange for Change) as an example. The motto, "writing that transforms," rings of truth. Which is just like saying, "education that changes." I've come to learn that writing on a consistent basis is therapeutic. And you will get the same type of remedy with any other form of education, as long as it's done consistently.

There's been hundreds of studies done that prove educated people make better decisions than non-educated people. I myself have gone to certain lengths to make sure that I continue to make wiser decisions in life. Mainly, because I have made writing (education) a staple in my life.

So if we as a society really want to start rehabilitating prisoners, in my opinion, this is the best route to take.

Because, yes, prison will always be prison. But education does make a difference. It brings about positive change.

**Tonight**  by Brian Rudolph


With both hands, I gently sway her face inches from mine. "I have never loved anyone like I love you," I reveal.

Krystal kisses me with enough electricity to power all of Washington, D.C.. After the sparks, she hugs me intensely and does not let go. Our time for my visit is about up.

I caress her thin shoulders and rest my head on top of her soft dark hair.  Softly, I ask her, "Are you ready?"


I dress myself in the wardrobe my stylist selected for tonight's black tie affair.  The pressed white pants with black pinstripes remind me of a zebra. The white jacket has shoulder pads like I am kicking for my high school football team again, instead of a night mingling with celebrities.

"You look sexy," Krystal compliments.

"I wish you could have seen my body twenty years ago, when I was your age."

"Are you kidding?  I did! I saw your first movie when I was sixteen.  It was love at first sight," Krystal giggles. "You had long golden hair then."

I laugh.  "I had a better stylist then, too."

Her giant blue eyes become glossy.  "You don't have to do this tonight. I know you truly love me.  I can wait."

I swallow my looming fear and replace it with a polished, brave face. "*I can't wait any longer . . . Three years of hiding . . . every day I am incomplete, when it is not you I wake up next to.  My daughter . . . Camille is old enough to understand now. I feel like a hypocrite and I need to finally set the example.  Tonight.*"


The blacked-out window partition in my limo rolls down.

"What's the plan, boss?"  Mark, my driver, asks.

"We need to rendezvous with my family and entourage for the gala.  Also, I'm starving. Can you sneak us into the drive-thru at The Grease Bucket?  I really want a bomb burger."

"No problem, boss."

"Oh . . . and Mark, please warn my better half to make sure my daughter is dressed *elegantly*, and not *sultry*.  She heard 'The Stone' will be there tonight."

"Sixteen year-olds.  What can you do, right?  So how was your therapy session?  You were in there a while, boss." Mark gives me a wink via the rearview.

I roll my eyes first, and the glass partition second.

I call Rachel, the press secretary, on one of my cellphones.

"Yes, VEEP?" Rachel answers promptly.

"I just emailed you my speech for tonight.  Please look it over for corrections, and have it set up," I instruct her.

"Did you make some revisions?"

"Rachel, this is a whole new speech."

"VEEP, did I miss a meeting? When was there time for a rewrite?" Rachel's voice carries confusion.

"Many days, I have wept in the bathroom while working on it. All in the hope that one day I could read it and live the life I want. Rachel, this is why you were hired two years ago. You have experience with this."

"No, no, no, no, VEEP! Please don't do this tonight! This gala is a charity event for the freaking *L.G.B.T.* You will be redirecting attention from them to you. *Not* good," Rachel advises.

"This can work. I added in the speech that it is their courage that inspires me. Tonight, I will be announcing my divorce and my affair with my therapist, Dr. Krystal Bach. So please work your magic," I declare, and hang up.


My family and I maneuver through the red carpet and the paparazzi. During the many photo ops with my family, I have my daughter stand in between us, so I can shield the slit in her dress that embarrassingly travels way above her right knee into her thigh.

Upon entry, Camille insists on hunting down "The Stone."

Jay "The Stone" Wilson was voted *People's* Sexiest Man of the Year for the last two years. He is a former T.V. wrestler, who is now a popular action movie star.

I grimace as Camille's pale skin shines through the slit of her red gown as she walks away.

"We have to talk," I whisper in my spouse's ear.

"Look, Sam: Camille gave me a profile glance for approval. I didn't see the slit. She is smart, like you."

"It's not that. Tonight I'm announcing my affair and our divorce. We have to tell Camille now."

Wide eyes stare back at me. "Sam, we agreed to wait for Camille to go to college. That's only a year away. You will be throwing her into a media *frenzy*. Me as well!"

"I can't wait any longer. Camille can handle it," I say, definitively.

"Here? Tonight, of all nights? I thought we had an agreement, Sam?"

"Our original agreement was that this marriage was a power move for our political careers. And that either of us could end it when we chose to," I reminded.

"That was over twenty *years* ago, Sam! Who would have thought we would make it to the *White House*?"

"*I did* . . .," I offer a long kiss on the lips. "You've been a great parent, friend, and confidant. I will always care about you. But . . .," I wipe a tear from my eye, "But I need you to wait in the green room, where we can explain this to Camille."

I am given a solemn nod as the gravity of the situation sinks in. I grab the first flute of champagne I can find before I start my search for Camille.

My military advisor, General Boon, flanks me. "Finn, we need more resources to apprehend Kalerman. He is far too dangerous to be allowed to sneak out of the Middle East and rebuild his terrorist network."

"General Boon, do you want me to put on my uniform again and join the hunt? I could use a change of scenery," I joke.

Boon offers a fake laugh, "Finn, you were always a better mouthpiece in public relations than you were at being a soldier."

"Flattery will get you nowhere with me, General."

He slaps the back of my shoulder, "I just need you to promote support from the right people."

I nod and scan the ballroom for Camille. In my peripheral, I see her with "The Stone." "I'll see what wheels I can grease for you, General."

When I turn around, Boon slaps my butt like a football player. "Finn, don't forget that crazy night in '85. I didn't," he says with a devilish grin and wink.

I look around and relax. No one heard or saw him. One drunken night in 1985, during our military service, we had *ménage-a-trois* with a local girl. I was young, dumb, and blowing off steam because preparing for battle is a scary thing. Boon likes to remind me, when he needs a favor.

"Geez, Boon. How could I forget? She was some dish, right?" I offer him a salute goodbye.

I place my empty flute on a server's platter and pick up a fresh one. On my way towards Camille, Senator John Abel signals me with his arms wide open, fifteen feet away.

"Shark, my bill on education: I made the modifications you wanted. When can I expect you to announce your support? If not, the bill will die," Abel pleas.

A pretty young server offers us *hors d'oeuvres* from her platter. "Kobe beef dumplings?"

Abel and I take one each and thank her. Before she hustles away, she gives me a sly grin, with a wink. "My pleasure, Shark."

"Senator, you're right. I'll tell Rachel to put it on my agenda. Please keep up the good work." I shake his hand and walk to Camille.

Camille is one of *many* young ladies fawning over "The Stone." He spots me and offers his hand, "Wow, the Shark! Looking good. It is such an honor to meet you."

"The honor is all mine. I'm a big fan," I return his compliments and shake his hand.

"Would you consider returning to the silver screen? I'm about to start in a trilogy—*The Clone Disruption*—and with you as a co-star, sales would go through the roof!"

"So kind of you to offer, but my schedule is full for now. If you could please excuse us," I gesture to Camille and grab her hand, "I need a moment with my daughter."

Camille blushes and waves goodbye as I escort her away.

Rachel approaches and falls in stride with us, "You look *radiant*, Camille," she praises.

"Thank you, Rachel. You look stunning, also," Camille responds.

"VEEP, your table guests are anticipating your arrival. They made *outrageous* donations to dine at your table. Way beyond the normal twenty-grand-a-plate entrance fee. We promised an hour and a half with them, plus your speech."

"Is the speech ready?"

"I have it loaded on the teleprompters. You are all set. Plus, I still have the original speech loaded, if you change your mind," Rachel glances at Camille like a lost puppy, and then back at me. "VEEP, you sure about this?"

"Yes, I'm sure. I will join my table after we talk to Camille. Thanks, Rachel."

"What is Rachel talking about with your speech?" Camille asks as Rachel walks away.

In the green room, we tell her everything. In chronological order. Our marriage was based on career motivations, founded with friendship and respect. The last few years I had spent falling in love with Krystal. How I wanted to start a new life with her. Our belief that Camille is strong and mature enough to support us.

Camille laughs at first, in shock, maybe. Then she cries. We share a long, enduring family hug until the crying subsides.

"I understand," Camille finally says.

"I love you more than anything in the world," I tell her.

With concern in her tone, she asks me, "Are you sure you want to do this tonight?"

I stroke Camille's golden hair, "I have to be a role model for you and be honest with everyone. I need to live my life, the way God intended it."

We leave the green room and head back to the ballroom. Before I depart from my family to the heavy donors at my table, Camille squeezes my arm and asks, "Do you think 'The Stone' is gay?"

"I don't know. Why?" I ask.

"There are so many gay people here," Camille responds.

"Well, Camille, this gala is a charity for lesbians, gays, bisexuals, and trans-genders. So . . . maybe?"

I take my seat at my table. Jupiter and Sabrina Willis, the superb tennis star sisters, sit across from me. Also the retired, gay,

NBA center Carson Jullians; Kevin, that gay Olympic diver I read about in the newspapers;  and Michael Georges, the popular bi-sexual rock star. The Olympic triathlete, now called 'Kate,' sits on my left, next to the famous T.V. host Hellen and her girlfriend.  Jamy Winehome, the Grammy-winning singer famous for repeated arrests, rehab, and sex-tapes sits on my right. They all toast my arrival and greet me.

I entertain their questions.  Sports? Yes, I played soccer and football in high school, but only soccer in college.  My four years of military service was in public relations.9 Yes, I was in Desert Storm, briefly.  Afterwards, I starred in five feature films, a series called *Sharkteeth*, where I was a surfer who was hunted by sharks.  With my last name being Finn, I formed a surfer apparel company called Shark Finn Wear, hence the nickname.  I married my business partner. We started a career in politics. My greatest accomplishment? Camille, no doubt.

During conversations, Jamy Winehome's hand flirts with my leg under the table.  She whispers in my ear, "I spent almost a quarter million to sit next to you tonight.  I want to see you after the gala. Bring a friend, if you want." She teases with a wink and licks her lips.

I remove her hand and thank her for her large donation.

It's getting close to my speech, and I am getting close to declaring my love for Krystal.  I imagine seeing her daily in my bedroom, walking hand-in-hand in a park, or enjoying a romantic vacation together.  No more hiding and brief visits. I deserve such happiness. Don't we all?

The P.A. system takes over the soft music.

"Ladies and gentlemen, at this time I present to you our guest of honor:  the vice president of the United States, Samantha 'The Shark' Finn!"

At the podium, I can see my daughter wave with a huge smile.  She gives me two thumbs up.

**Wake Up!**  by Parnell Smith


No comfy bed!

Soft pillows!

Or Downy washed sheets!

It's just us two,

Walking down a busy street;

"Slow down man!"

"The lights red!"

"You don't see that truck?"

          You're walking in a daze

             My brother

          You need to wake up!

Yeah, yeah I know.

You say it every time.

(I'm cool dude,

I got something on my mind.)


On your mind,

while standing on two feet.

It ain't cool this day and age,

to be walking while you sleep!


There's smoke on the horizon.

A fire's burning,

that much is true.

Hands in the air!

Choke holds!

Toy trucks too!

What does America,

want the Black Man to do?


"Boom! Boom!"

"Pow—Pow—Pow!"

What in tarnation is going on now?

Another minority down!

Had his hands up.

It's time to be shaken,

So we can wake up!

Hey, pops!

I don't smell no smoke,

and where's this fire you see?

You must think I'm lame, dude,

talking stupid jive to me.

This K2, Molly, and needles,

they don't define me.

Much smarter than what you think I be!

Trix are 4 kids!

And kids are 4 trix!

Pay attention old school,

This is Generation X!

Galaxy 7 + the iPod,

we're that damn smart.

Why, we're the next best thing to God!

Now!

Can you smell?

Do you see?

If I'm asleep,

just let me be.

Old age got you shaking,

Waking up ain't 4 me!

The people are full of rage,

their hearts are about to burst.

Your days are filled with getting high,

and drinking to quench a thirst.

Look around, brah,

Where's your homey at?

If not in prison,

they're dead from somebody's gat!

The girls you knew,

disease done took them home.

Somebody,

help my people open their eyes.

Please, Lord,

Turn the lights on!

They say:

"The best part of waking up,

  Is Folgers in your cup!"

               Wow, It's only Cristal and Sizzurp

                    they drunk.

                Will this generation ever,

                    Wake up?

ISIS on the rise!

Trump and Hillary telling lies!

One will win, that's no surprise!

Obama's surely out the door!

What, I ask you,

is America waiting for?


Fires, floods, and storms are here,

ripping this country a brand new rear;

Kardashians getting ripped off,

their daddy went and cut it off,

                oooh . . .

P.D.A by Bob and Drew,

What's America coming to?

My mom's doped out,

my dad's in jail,

me and my siblings are catching hell!


Gang Bang!

Dope We Slang!

Bullets Flying!

Hitting everybody and anything!


"People Crying"

What the Fuck?!

We still

sit around,

pretending like

there's no need for us

to wake up!

**The Last Page** by Catherine LaFleur

The sun is blinding on this Spring Everglades morning. I hurry along on the way to meditation class because today, Dada, *brother*, a traveling monk, is coming to our prison. He stands in front of the building where our class will be held; his bright orange robes flap in the breeze. Dada looks like an exotic peony as he waves to the line of inmates pushing past to the recreation yard. A few prisoners stop, confused at the sight of this colorful character, and wave back. But no one comes over to find out who Dada is. Only the twelve members of the class step out of the crowd.

Once inside the classroom, I sit in lotus position and clear my mind. Today I will be coloring outside the lines. Dada guides me with his voice to a forest glade with a calm pool. A droplet of water plinks into the pool at intervals. As I sit beside the pool, a book appears upon my lap. Upon opening the book, an image of a person whom I love forms on the page. I follow Dada's spoken mantra silently in my head while gazing at the person's face.

*May this person be whole,*

*May this person be healthy,*

*May this person be happy,*

*May this person find peace.*

A drop of water falls into the pool and I turn the page. Another person's image forms, except this is a person I've had a

conflict with. I repeat the mantra: *whole . . . healthy . . . happy . . .*
*peaceful.* Dada leads me through several pages and I release each
person until I come to the last page. The image which forms is
indistinct, dark, and murky. And suddenly there it is, the tiniest
twinge, like a tickle in the back of the throat right before tears begin
to fall.

I can't recall too much of what happened. His face and
clothes are a blank to me. I only see the back of his head on the
page. Thick hair trailing slightly over his collar. Of course he had a
knife. They usually have something—a knife, a gun, brute strength,
or the element of surprise.

He doesn't speak at first, just punches me in the face. I fall
down onto stuffed trash bags. One breaks as I hit it. Next, he's
holding the blade to my face, just under my left eye. I try to
remember what I learned at a rape awareness seminar I attended in
college.

*Don't resist.*

*Don't struggle.*

*Don't fight.*

*Don't do anything which might cause your attacker to kill*
*you.*

My skirt rips along with a part of my mind, which flies away
from my body. The assault seems to drag on and on, but is really

over in minutes. I'm safe in my detached refuge watching what is happening to my body lying on the ground.

I can't feel anything in this moment, not even anger. That comes later. I'm just relieved it looks like he's going to be done soon. He groans and goes limp. It's over. I snap back into my body. He's heavy and leaning on my chest. Can't catch my breath. I try and push him off. Then, his fingertips brush across my face, closing my eyelids as he turns my head away to the wall. I'm waiting for the blade on my throat, but he pushes hard on my shoulders and gets to his feet. Then he's gone.

The cold air slices my body. Rolling to my knees, I push my skirt back down and hold the torn edges together. The car isn't too far away. I fumble with my keys and manage to unlock the door. Finally, I get the car open and collapse into the passenger seat, crawl over behind the steering wheel, and engage the automatic locks. And I sit and sit and sit, until I start screaming, shaking, and banging the car with my fists.

But that was years ago, and today I am sitting by a calm pool of water. Droplets hit the surface one by one. Like an old soldier, I am looking at this wound—clear of shrapnel and long healed. Almost. *Almost*. I am saying the words with gritted teeth, and turning the last page.

*May this person be whole,*
*May this person be healthy,*

*May this person be happy,*

*May this person be at peace.*

**Change: The Power of its Momentum**  by Waldo Hewitt


Change is an alteration—to make different; vary.
Alterations in our evolutionary experiences have taught us values.
A static world would strangle humanity with stagnation. Change for
the mere purpose of comparing and contrasting, at the minimum,
cultivates understanding.  Lessons learned in the changes of the
American people inspired significant changes in the toleration of
racial differences. Change is the food of the hungry stomach of
dissatisfaction, and dissatisfactions in themselves hint at
deficiencies.  The clouds of change have rained hate, love, war, and
peace on humanity for a long time. But it is by living through these
storms and sunny days that man has learned what material is best
suited for the making of his culture.

Delete changes from the caterpillar, and it becomes a tree-
clinging, twelve-legged pest for an eternity.  This example of
stagnation would be an injustice to the majestic butterfly; Man
would never know the butterfly's beauty.  A metamorphosis from
one state to one of greater beauty is inherent not only in the
caterpillar, but also in the development of humans, societies, and
cultures otherwise locked in a static world.

"United we stand; Divided we fall," is one of this country's
mottos, but a static 19th century would have kept the manifestation
of this ideal from the American people.  The huge biceps of

segregation in the old days colored communities black and white. Change kept this condition from being warehoused in our schools, businesses, marketplaces, and politics (what were the chances of a black President in the days of segregation?). The 21st century may have witnessed some very questionable police shootings of black civilians, lighting a fuse to the Black Lives Matter movement, but these incidents didn't burn with the kind of injustices of the 17th, 18th, and 19th centuries, unless one thinks these police shootings are reasonably comparable to the massacre of black civilians in the Florida town called Rosewood, in 1923, where homes and churches owned by blacks were burned, and the entire community was chased away never to return (see Gannon). Or to the killings in Memphis, Tennessee in 1866, where a white mob joined police officers in murdering at least 46 innocents and injuring 285 (Manasseh), or similar incidents in New Orleans, Louisiana; Pulaski, Tennessee; Opelousas, Louisiana; Eutaw, Alabama; Laurens, South Carolina; and Camilla, Georgia—all in that same year. At least the 21st century police shootings raised a public debate of legality.

Historian Michael Gannon reminds us that the lynchings and racial mob attacks of previous centuries were like a form of legalized terrorism: "[T]he brutal lynching of Claude Neal in Jackson County in 1934 drew the attention of the nation. Rarely were those responsible prosecuted" (Gannon 379).

The proponents of the modern day slavery theory (see Alexander), argue that the government is part of a mass incarceration movement today.  Assuming this theory is true, for the sake of argument (I believe there's some truth to it), the choice of incarceration over murder is the lesser of two evils, because life is preserved and valued, and the criminal class plays an active role in their own imprisonment.  Furthermore, protestors have a voice today, one that Gannon makes clear would have gotten them lynched in old America: "Black Floridians knew their place in society, and few dared to step outside of it" (Gannon 379). Today's protestors unite from all classes and races.  It is highly unlikely such a picture could have occurred anywhere in America even a hundred years ago. Did blacks and whites even fight "side by side" in the Civil War? The power change has had on race relations cannot be denied.

Although I've changed addresses from "society" to the Department of Corrections, I've experienced change on a much subtler level that gives me, too, something to thank change for.  Through the power of reading and writing (made possible through the selfless service of *Exchange for Change* and the lessons and grace of meditation masters Lawrence Huff, Gurumayi Chidvilasananda, and Pir Saheb Mastwaar Qalandar), change transformed my *perception* of myself, my country, society, and even this "prison."  The person I used to be at the start of my incarceration, nicknamed "Doughboy," started a slow process of death around June 26<sup>th</sup>, 2001. That night, I thought I was on my way to Hell. But today, my perception is that that night was the start of my "prison pilgrimage." Coming from a community that held an unwritten rule of segregation—Hollywood ("Liberia"), Florida, where you find streets are named after Confederate generals—my view of self and the world was founded on little education, so I read every history book in the prison library I could find, and studied Plato's complete works. I learned about the Greeks' relationship with ancient Egypt, one that showed the most famous Greek philosophers were students of the Egyptians—a people as black as the rest of Africa. A study of the relationships between Romans, Greeks, Egytians, and the rest of the East proved to me that the race problem of America and Europe did not exist in those times. I concluded that racism was culturally bred. It was inherent in no one. The world made racism. A baby is not born that way. People were not born to hate—they were *taught* to hate. In the same respect, I saw that my own problem was cultural, and that my old lifestyle was not a virtuous as I thought it was. I had taken the easy path. The hard workers were the disciplined people who educated themselves and contributed to society. I used to chide my school boy peers for being "square" when the worked hard; now I wanted to be square, too.

The meditation teachers gave me the formula upon which to prove I was not "Doughboy." I followed the old Ancient Greek (by way of Egypt) ideal—"man, know thyself"—feeling I had been misguided on the question of identity, and trusted the teachers. In the laboratory of my cell, I watched the practice of their meditation instructions as it deteriorated the greed, lust, hatred, and selfishness that the ghetto had planted within me. I experienced the theory that meditation mystically formed self control and connected the practitioner with other people, in such a way that their pain or joy could be felt. Slowly, I cultivated more patience, contentment, compassion, and insight into my view of the world and its race problem.

The trauma of growing up in the ghetto had left many scars on my heart. Daily, I had witnessed prejudice (from my side of the streets), shootouts, fights, and all types of drama. But the meditations erased these wounds. Recent research on meditation shows that the portion of the brain that responds to physical pain— the *anterior cingulate cortex*—also responds to emotional pain. Meditation has taught me that bad thoughts are powerless without the food of attention. I keep the mind under observation— "mindfulness"—and when I recite, mentally, the "words of power" provided by the Master, the negativity that emerges from the mind starves from detachment.

The momentum of meditation has the power to reshape a rough rock from the 'hood and grow a rose from the concrete, proving that the condition of any mind is cultural. Using sophisticated imaging techniques, scientists are finding an interesting difference between the right and left sides of the *prefrontal cortex* (which lies behind your forehead). Brain activity on the right *prefrontal cortex* is associated with depression and being uptight; the left is associated with happiness and relaxation. In studies done on meditators and non-meditators by Harvard professors, guess whose left *prefrontal cortex* showed more activity? Meditators, of course. I understand exactly what the scientists have demonstrated, and without a microscope and the study of others. The meditation states or stations are, in part, peace, tranquility, contentment, bliss, and union with something "greater" than the individual, all conditions uncharacteristic of a mind forcibly separated from its loved ones.

Visitacion Valley Middle School adopted a meditation program in 2007 and saw significant results in its rowdy students who were from a neighborhood where gunfire was as common as birds chirping. The school is located in San Francisco, and was one of the most troubled schools in the Bay Area. According to Professor David L. Kirp's January 12th, 2014 article, "Meditation Transforms Roughest San Francisco Schools," in the *San Francisco Chronicle*:

In years past, these students were largely out of control, frequently fighting in the corridors, scrawling graffiti on the walls and cursing their teachers. Absenteeism rates were among the city's highest and so were suspensions. Worn-down teachers routinely called in sick.

Unsurprisingly, academics suffered. The school tried everything, from counseling and peer support to after-school tutoring and sports, but to disappointingly little effect (Kirp). In the same article, Professor Kirp points out the changes after meditation programs were instituted. In the first year of "Quiet Time," as they titled the program, suspensions fell by 45 percent. Within four years, the suspension rate was amongst the lowest in the city. Daily attendance rates climbed to 98 percent, well above the city average. In the annual "California Healthy Kids Survey," these middle school students recorded the highest happiness levels in San Francisco. Similar results from adopting "Quiet Time" occurred in other Bay Area schools as well, like Burton High School (Kirp).

Meditation's "opening up" of my heart prepared me to receive not just the lessons, but the compassion that *Exchange for Change* facilitators brought to Dade C.I., providing embodiments of the bliss and love I experienced within, and proving my conclusion that racism was cultural. Most of the *Exchange* facilitators were white Americans who sacrificed free time to help prisoners better themselves via "writing it out." These people descended on the compound like angels. Indeed, they represented a sharp contrast from the old white America depicted in history books. Conceptually concluding that racism was cultural was not as educational as witnessing a part of white America who must have come from the cultivation of equality, love, and compassion.

The tides of change push on all the barriers set up by the past, personal and national. It's unlikely that an incarcerated black inmate could have seen *Exchange for Change* angels in the early 19th century, just as it's unlikely that I would have found the power of meditation in the 'hood. The power of change had not sprouted conditions for something like *Exchange for Change* in the early 19th century. And had I not changed my environment, and eventually my perception, and had I been left in my old neighborhood, the language of violence, deception, and hatred would have filled every breath in my lungs. Although the 'hood is here in prison, via meditation, reading, and writing, I was able to transform my perception and see a university, a temple, and classrooms. My environment may have changed in a negative way, but my perception changed in such a positive way. I could see the good in this environment. Perception is the key—perception shaped by the momentum of meditation and the changes in America's race relations.

Where I used to awake to a fat blunt, now I wake up to the breathing and mental chanting exercises of meditation, and the writing assignments of *Exchange for Change*. God bless change!

For Further Reading:

Alexander, Michelle. *The New Jim Crow: Mass Incarceration in the Age of Colorblindness*. New York, The New Press, 2010.

Benson, Herbert, and Miriam Z. Klipper. *The Relaxation Response*. Revised ed., New York, HarperCollins, 2000.

Gannon, Michael. *The New History of Florida*. Gainesville, FL, U. of Florida Press, 1996.

Kirp, David L. "Meditation Transforms Roughest San Francisco Schools." *The San Francisco Chronicle*, 12 Jan. 2014, www.sfgate.com/opinion/openforum/article/ Meditation-transforms-roughest-San-Francisco-5136942.php. Accessed 15 June 2017.

Manasseh, Tamar. "America's Violent Past and the Question of Race." *The Final Call* , 24 Jan. 2011, www.finalcall.com/artman/publish/Perspectives_1/ article_7569.shtml.  Accessed 8 July 2017.

**When My Spirit Grows Faint Unshaken Faith** by Allen L. Dorsey, Sr.

I have been a Christian since childhood, but my faith had been an easy one—no real trials or tribulations to test my dependence on Christ!

Only a few people knew I was experiencing anxiety and the depth of it. But it was in this place of isolation that I finally heard God calling me into a closer relationship with Him.

And he answered. Faithfully, God began revealing himself to me as I called out frantic pleas for help. The Lord directed me to His Holy Word to rescue the comfort and grace I needed to sustain me during my walk in the wilderness of loneliness, isolation and separation, from my family and friends. "Seeing then that we have a great High Priest who has passed through the heavens, Jesus Christ, the Son of God, let us hold fast our confession . . ." (Hebrews 4:14-16). And this gave me the courage to persevere and continue to seek His comfort through this rough journey in my life. So as I cross my Red Sea and walk through the desert, I will keep my eyes upon the Lord.

I realized that He had kept me from the hands of death during my many deployments around the world. So, this little "time out" period to reflect on His greatness in my life over the past half century is nothing compared to the first half of my voyage through life.

When I feel my feet slipping, His unfailing love supports me upright, and when anxiety and depression try to creep upon me, His consolation brings me great joy. This allows me to smile each day and be Thankful for all the blessings He has bestowed upon me: sixteen beautiful children, a loving wife, over 40 grandchildren, loving and nurturing parents, 17 siblings, and numerous other family and friends. I can't help but be overjoyed at the life I have lived thus far. A little down time and rest is good for the soul, to complete the rest of my journey into the Promise Land.  Psalm 23:3 says, "He restores my soul. He leads me in the paths of righteousness for His name's sake."

I can never say that the Lord ever "Shook The Spoon" on *me*, as he has prepared a table for me in the presence of my enemies; He has anointed my head with oil and my cup runneth over.  I am full of life and my purpose is to pay it forward to the less fortunate who have received less than a full spoon all their life. I refuse to "Shake the Spoon" of God's grace!

**Demolishment Needed**  by Luis Hernandez


You never visited . . . where were you? Knowing you was
elusive. Hate abided—you didn't even know where I
resided. I looked for you in the cabinets where I used
to hide, the only ones by my side were darkness and
roaches. I searched the closets, the rooms and the roof.
I crawled the whole back yard, digging with burning red
wet hands. Master hate whipping my back, causing me to dig
deeper, like a dog looking for the bone.

In my house hate punched holes in the walls that never
spoke, but they felt every stroke—every dose of sadness,
loneliness, bitterness, was forced. Time bombs replaced
the emptiness of the holes left deep in my soul. Torment,
terror decorated the house.

No sunshine coming through hostility boarded the windows.
Rain mingled with my tears as it poured through the holes
of the roof.  Dry days were rare.

No foundation—the cracks and uneven floor kept my
knees scarred. In vain I treaded carefully over anger
mines that shook me like a 6.5, I trembled for

years.

Where were you . . . when this house was ruled
by the  dictator? The angry, driven, iron fist kept
my body aching. The rules were like attempting the
vault without the pole. Every day the scepter broke
me like a rebellious mule.

Maybe I ran from you like running from my dads
machete. The raging sharp blade severed father's
arms of protection. You were silent, while hate
screamed in my ear. You weren't there, but it was
always near. What about you ever felt scared . . .
maimed instead of welcomed?

Ending, none in sight.  Coming to save me was a
dream because the ones who were supposed to help
me . . . helped me deteriorate like a condemned,
dilapidated crack house consumed from the
inside.

Demolishment, needed for a new edification.
Completely leveled for a great foundation.
Removing anger, hate, bitterness. Embracing the best

tools of education.

Love is building action.

The healing to the holes left open from the extraction.


It expelled the detested dictator. Extinguished the

reign of anger. Evicted the oppression,

giving the pole and the push to overcome the past.


Living in years of hopeless contrition. Ignoring the heart's

petition. Indifferent to the suffering of an aimless

and wandering soul. Turning fear into courage—turning

the house into a home for those who have never

felt or known that . . . Love is the beginning of

deep soul sanitation.

Welcome home.

**Sandwich Crusts**  by Christopher Malec

A fall afternoon in Florida often casts a sky blue smile of
clarity at rains passed, as if they're never to return. Birds interrupt
the smooth panorama in a glide as if swimming without causing a
ripple, instigating the notion that it may have been them who made
Newton question the laws of gravity. I took note of this as I sat on a
withered prison picnic bench, and stared at the brown paper bag
directly in front of me with a deeper question in mind: Should I eat
the sandwich inside crust first or not?

Sandwich crusts . . . They're the one part of a meal most
people never give a thought to. Eaten aimlessly, bitten off as they
come, and ending up as the last thing devoured by default; the
handle on the sandwich. Or, they're ripped off the sandwich like an
unwanted all-natural wrapper of blandness, fated to be tossed
away without considering all the starving children in Somalia we see
on the infomercials. In both cases, sandwich crusts are the extras of
any lunch stage cast.

Back when I was five or six, my mom tip-toed the tightrope
of the poverty line, and yet still had difficulties keeping the state's
assistance. In the mid-90s standard of living, as long as there was
some balance to rely on you didn't need the Welfare Department's
help. It didn't matter if there was still margin for error or a fall;
others were in more of a need. The Department took its safety net

from under us. When it whipped it away, free school lunches went with it.

Luckily, the old girl's job was as a day cook at a sports bar. For all pragmatic purposes, there was no reason to go hungry, even if the rest of life's comforts dwindled away like the last embers of a firework I didn't want to see cease to explode. So to curb the embarrassment of being unable to eat at lunch with the other kids, my mom sent me to school with brown bags transparent from greasy stolen goods so I could have some semblance of dignity, in spite of the sting from Uncle Sam's most recent slap.

My initial expectation was that I'd be chided like the other kids who brought home-packed, would-be gourmets to school. Either jokes about living in a cardboard box, or having a goody two-shoes, snotty-stuck-up type of parenting were the extremes which kids who ate from home had to endure, and I knew I wasn't going to be subject to the latter. My shoes and hair told that story.

The reception I received was quite different. Moms made the most out of every two slices of bread she had to work with. Between them I found everything from a full order of chicken tenders slathered in honey and BBQ sauce, to a quarter-pounder decked with grilled onions, Swiss cheese, mushrooms, and A-1, to grilled Tilapia sprinkled with lemon and topped with tartar. And if I was lucky, a filet mignon with god knows what else she managed to mix in. I couldn't focus on class third hour every day waiting on lunch, and the other kids were either jealous or impressed depending on what a six-year-old's

sneer means. Whatever it was, I got spared the jokes, and instead got pleas for a

bite.

And me, well I just wasn't having it. Even at that age. Wasn't nothing personal, but if your mom picked you up in a fancy luxury sedan the commercials just featured last week, or you had on a pair of shoes I ogled from a storefront display the way Tom did Jerry, the chances of you getting a bite of my sandwich were slim to none. And slim slipped with the welfare department's safety net.

But I couldn't outright deny a hungry child over and over without guilt's tick sucking on my consciousness, so I had to come up with another way to get around the other little booger-brains' queries. It was by chance that I'd figured it out, too. I started eating in far corners of the cafeteria, where other home-lunch eaters migrated to escape the majority's disdain for their individuality. Either that or shame, but I can't say I was experiencing shame in the least. One of my regular potential siphoners came to find me one day, but by the time he homed in on me, my sandwich was nearly gone. Out of sheer admiration for the Christopher Columbus-style search he had to have embarked on to find me, I offered up a bite for his trouble. Surprisingly, he declined. His reason: I had bitten off of the sandwich already. He still stuck to the table under the pretense of light banter to disguise his motive, but the light bulb over my head was a burning sun; I now had my out.

I took to ducking into any corner I could to rapidly bite off the crust of my sandwiches, so that by the time anyone asked for one, it was too late. The sandwich had officially been contaminated on every side. Too bad, so sad; should've arrived sooner.

As I grew, the tendency stayed. I ate every sandwich crust first; middle last. But the reason no longer remained the same, just the habit. Like the guys who get out of a Florida prison and knock on the table at the end of every meal, or the smoker who quits, but still wants to pack everyone else's box of cigarettes for them. An homage to a reprieve once savored in the midst of a bitter experience; the one part of the memory's palette that remained numb as you chewed the present into a swallowed past.

By the time I was in my teens, I gravitated towards people like me. People with the scars of governmental slaps decorating them like Halloween masks, roaming the streets, trick-or-treating for sweet cash and sour consciousness. At the end of every night, we were a pack; a family. No hierarchy, no dictatorship. No one was better than the next. A bottom feeder is a bottom feeder whether he has a shell or a fin to rely on. So in a young, narrow-minded misfit's philosophy, we were all each other had. In my mind, I had finally found the people worth sharing a sandwich with.

I never kicked the crust idiosyncrasy. I think at that point it was a mild form of OCD in my psyche. So rather than try to quit, I made it a point to offer up a bite to any of my homeboys, lest anyone should feel neglected. Everyone knew my method; no one ever questioned it, like Kramer's hairstyle on the show *Seinfeld*. It just was what it was.

As the years went on, I added one more exception to the rule: Girlfriends. If they were willing to put up with my lifestyle, my habits, and my shit (which amounted to dealing with a lit stick of dynamite next to a gas pump), then they were worthy of some of my sandwich, though I doubt any of them ever understood the implications of what that bite meant; of just how much I had accepted them emotionally. Owners hardly ever reward their cats for leaving dead vermin on their doorsteps, and I'm sure the cats wonder why the hell they're being reproached for leaving prize game as an honor to their beloved.

It came to me somewhere around that time that our psychology affects our behaviors and develops tendencies, and that maybe those tendencies, in turn, develop part of our psychologies as well. For me, sandwich crusts had become more than a memento of my past; more than a token of acceptance into my inner circle. They had become symbolic of the philosophy that if you get the boring work and tasteless sides of life out of the way, all that's left are the meatier moments of existence. So that's what I did.

Despite living a bottom feeder's existence, I still handled my illegitimate responsibilities, helped pay the bills, and survived on way better means than my mom's paycheck could have furnished, albeit in a felonious manner. Once all that was out of the way, I enjoyed my habits, local parties, and whatever whim my friends and I pursued. I was lighting firecrackers under Mr. Sam's rocking chair. I just didn't see Lady Justice peeking from under her blindfold. When she caught up to me, they took turns lashing me against the post. That seemed to become a recurring event throughout my young adult life. I tried to show I was tired of walking tightropes without a net. I preferred to trapeze over the gap, regardless of what the ringleader wanted.

I wound up in and out of juvie joints, on to the county jail, catching one prison bid, and then another with more time than the sun is projected to exist, all before I could purchase a legit bottle of liquor. Back during my first bid, moms had managed to leave a cigarette burning in the ashtray one night that wound up consuming all my worldly things in an insatiable blaze worthy of the five o'clock news. At least, that's where I watched it.

The only things that remained were memories and tendencies; an abstract journal of existing, etched onto my soul with the tips of blunts, chipped nail ends from one night stands, and glass shattered from bottles long since emptied.

Throughout all that though, I still observed the sandwich crust ritual. At first, it was for all the same reasons, but you learn early on in the pen that almost no one has your best interests at heart—it's something you just manage to live with it as you suspect and see everyone you encounter through Sherlock's magnifying glass. Before long I was viciously tearing away crusts again without regard. My first few years turned out to be pretty lonely.

I even started to avoid calling friends or family. All those people I lit a firecracker for, and shared the laugh with; those people I never called out as I took those lashings against the post. They stayed on the porch; I hung lifelessly, held by the tethers that kept my hands bound. The tethers looked strangely close to the net that had been taken from under me in the first place. The whole time I wondered how I ever offered the people on the porch a bite.

Time cleaned and dressed my wounds slowly, and eventually I found a few people I could give a measure of trust. I began to offer a piece of my sandwiches to some beforehand again. This time it even came with an added benefit: a gauging tool. If the person started to look for it or expect it, I knew it was time to put the social match head to that leech and retreat into my shell again. It signifies a personality that is probably clinging for a handout; baggage you should've left behind before you boarded the bus to hell. It actually turned out to be a good determinant too, yielding highly reliable results.

All the vacillation of tendencies started to tear away at my subconscious though, right around the same time I tore the seal off the envelope revealing a denial on my first appeal. The next slap came from the hands on the clock that sits above every prisoner's head: the halo of impermanence. Every tick was a realization of wasted seconds. I stopped eating the crusts first.

For the longest, I found myself in a solemn, somnambulistic state. I slogged through the tick throes of despair. I was uneven; unbalanced.

It wasn't until about a year and a half ago that I really started to knock on reality's door again. We had lunch once, as I sat on the rec-yard picnic bench strapped with a lunch bag smuggled from the show hall, and infested with more roaches than Joe's apartment. It was a luxury here compared to what's served on the regular food trays, believe it or not. A recent turn of events, and the right legal literature had divulged a possibility that the old net still hung from the ledge below the tightrope. If I played the alleys right and found the proper avenue, I might be able to climb back up and try to cross the right way this time. All hope wasn't lost; the ticks from that halo of impermanence grew fainter. I just needed a chance to ruminate on my situation.

For lunch, the paper bag uniformly held two bologna sandwiches, a peanut butter sandwich, two cookies, and a couple packets of mustard. Reality looked at my first sandwich expectantly, as if it desired a bit of it. I realized though, that what I was getting was a nudge; an insistence that it was time to wake up. I thought of those same bags my mom sent me to school with. I picked up the bologna and ate the crust first. Someone came around a short time later, and I offered him a piece of one of the other ones.

Existence has been more purposeful since then. We all get a bout of somnolence from time to time, but it never becomes a state for me anymore. Sure, I wonder sometimes what it would've been like if the finger-pointing bastard in a top hat ever offered me a bite. Maybe I'll ask when I make it across the tightrope.

**Open Black Sheep** by Kandis Lear

I'm an inner-racial woman. Have you seen?

The assumption of my skin is white, the texture of my hair appears black. I was conceived in only one sack. My future, I can't look back. Abandoned, busted open, belittled, belong? Bought at what price?

The doors that I read are (Black only) or (Whites only) it says. I didn't have a place to lay my head.

In bondage and free, I've lived with and without. My pouting days are over. My joyful shouts have just begun. This was me, this is me, this will forever be me. My past is my past. My present is just temporary. My future is where I am going, and that is what matters. It is not the life I'm dealt, it is how I live the life that counts.

This is me, and these are my shouts.

**Time and Circumstance**  by Israel Martinez


*Five Minutes After Test*

When the time came, it was impossible to do what I came for.  I looked him right in his young face and balked. The last thing I remember doing was running, unsure of what I was going to do next.  I never had to explain anything to him. It was only two words, but they were too difficult to speak.


*Fifty Minutes Before Test*

"I am telling you, Doctor Klein, it's not going to work."  The force of my assistant's voice was barely able to beat out all of the heavy machinery in the laboratory.  The two of us had been working together for ten years, and his lack of confidence of late had worn itself so thin that it was see-through.

"Christoph, please listen to me carefully," my own voice was hoarse from competing with my equipment, "I've sunk more than fifteen years' worth of research, all of it trial-and-error, into this.  I refuse to give up."

He stepped back from me and stared.  "K-klein . . . Kirk, I apologize. It's just, the work, it's . . . really demanding.  I appreciate what you are trying to do, more than you think." Tears welled up in his eyes.

The demand of the work, coupled with my incessant insistence on haste, had finally taken its toll. No man should have to work 14 hours a day for two years, every day, with breaks few and far between. Yet, the work we were doing was almost complete. I stared at Christoph, his blue eyes contrasted heavily with my worn-out brown ones. What was our age difference? Twenty years? Maybe more? I couldn't recall. It was evident that his mind was not as ready as my own for the task at hand.

"I've worked you too hard, Christoph. However, it is all for the sake of science. You have been my longest-running partner. Irreplaceable compared to all the dross the government usually sends." He reminded me much of myself, which may be why I worked him so hard. Especially at his age. Energetic, analytical, intelligent in almost everything he did. His drive for my own goals was right where I need it to be, but I was forgetting that he was not me, and so I worked the poor boy to the marrow. "You may take the rest of the day off. Please, don't argue with me about it."

The sight of his slacked jaw humored me, something I hadn't felt in a long while.

"In fact, take the rest of tomorrow off, as well."

"Doctor Klein, you can't be serious. I won't leave you alone to do—"

"That is an order. You mind is useless to me, anyway, without rest." The lie came easily enough. I needed Christoph gone to implement the device, and with progress so close to completion, I needed him gone anyway. He was too tired to realize any of this.

"Okay, Kirk. Thank you. Seriously, thank you. My girlfriend has been after me to spend more time with her. She has it in mind that I am fooling around with another woman. Silly jealousies because I am never home. She will really appreciate this." Before he finished his last sentence, he was out of his coat and out the lab doors, his voice trailing behind him.

*Nine Minutes Before Test*

Unbelievable—the last computations were simple binary anomalies. With a varying root equation, quantum travel was possible. This was my chance; Christoph would just have to forgive me. As I prepared the stasis pad, my thoughts went to one place: the winter of 2009, before I began my first semester towards my Master's degree in science. That year was when I made a terrible mistake and irreparably hurt the one I loved most. My fiancé found me sleeping with a close friend of hers. Her family never forgave me, and I never forgave myself. That moment of weakness had haunted me since.

The light of my life left because I didn't care about some darkness. At the time, I just shrugged it off—her loss. *She should never have accused me of cheating,* was my poor excuse of making good her accusation.

The whole experience left me a bitter man.  People distanced themselves, as I was no longer easy to deal with.  All my phonebook numbers were disconnected. The only positive thing was that my attitude allowed me to bull my way toward my research and force funding into the project.

The stasis pad hummed, alerting me to step up on it.  I punched the codes in the remote and activated the device, thinking *my sorrow will become my glory.*

*Three Minutes After Test*

I only had to say two words, and I would risk unraveling reality as I knew it.  I chose the moment right before I cheated on my fiancé. All I had to say to myself was, "I'm sorry."  That same plaid shirt I loved to wear back then was plastered over my sweaty form. I remember the moment, I was late for an important test for my class.  That shirt was my favorite because my fiancé had given it to me for my birthday that year, and I had been extremely flustered that I was ruining it.

I stepped up in his way and stared into his vibrant eyes, where a stupid, smug look sat upon his face.  A moment of consternation crossed his features and then a deep look of concentration. I opened my mouth to speak, but then snapped my jaw shut with an audible *clack* of my teeth. Before my past self could make any kind of connection, I ran away.

Two words left unspoken, because I feared changing the past, and I feared more that it would not change anything after I said my piece.

I stepped back on the stasis pad and punched in the return coordinates.

*Seven Minutes After Test*

I had been gone only minutes. *Did I really go that far for nothing?* There seemed to have been no changes within the lab. I couldn't even recall the event ever taking place in my past.

The lab doors slid open and Christoph entered mumbling expletives. "She thinks I am seeing another woman." He raised up his lab coat and jabbed his arms through the sleeves. "She says, and I quote, 'Why don't you go spend your supposed time off with the harlot you call *research* all day,' end quote. How dare she think that? It makes me want to make good on her assumptions." He began to busy himself on one of the lab computers. "It is very apparent that I do not need the time off, Doctor Klein. Let us continue our work."

I realized at that moment that I was wrong in my research. I was wrong in my approach to who needed to hear those words. I did not tell my younger self, because they were not meant for me to hear.  They were meant for Christoph. My obsession was about to put him in the same spot I had found myself in at the time.

I pulled a seat up to him and leaned on the desk.

"Christoph, please wait a moment. We need to talk."

It was only two words.  After seeing a past I could not alter, I now knew who to say them to.

**The Show** by Luis Aracena

*Did I look like that when I was 14? I mean, look at them—*
*they are practically babies!* My thoughts are interrupted by "Big P"
as he starts the "show," for lack of a better term, by informing the
teenage "babies" that prisons are not as bad as they imagine, but
rather much worse. I am not very proud of many things in my life. I
lived a life full of hurt, pain, anger, and crime, but being part of
*5000 Role Models* is one of the things I am most proud of, ever!

The *5000 Role Models* program is a partnership between the
Miami Dade County Public School System and the Department of
Corrections, where middle- and high-school minority students are
given an experience that they will never forget, *i.e., "Don't be like*
*me."*

When I first heard of this program my heart did a triple flip,
and I felt in my soul a surge of redemptive H.O.P.E.—that is, "help
other people escape" my fortune. Every Wednesday at 9:00 a.m., I
join a group of dedicated individuals, who, to me, are nothing but
heroes, and we take a walk to the visitor's park for an
approximately four-hour presentation as to why kids should make
better choices.  We are the example of what happens when they
make poor choices, and kids really listen and engage us as big
brothers instead of convicts, which always brings pleasure and joy
to my heart.

81

At approximately 1:00 p.m., the "show" ends and we always get the *thank you so much for your invaluable help* talk by DOC staff, only to be cursed at by the same staff at 1:15. Amazing!

The "show" has shown me how adults seem to always know it all, and how what happened to me could never happen to them, poor fools that they are; yet children grasp the urgency of the preventative message and they leave with information that is priceless and found nowhere else—information that may very well save their lives in the future.

I find a beautiful irony in this program; in the demons that are giving advice to angels in how to avoid coming to hell. It feels as if we are the demons, cheating Satan by depopulating Hades through our advice. My testimony pertains to gains, and redemption flows over my heart like ocean waves.

Every Wednesday as I leave the "show" behind me, the children's faces stay with me as a reminder that I can still make a difference in other people's lives, contrary to popular belief. Satan is the system, prison is hell, we are the demons, and children are angels; how do I make a difference in these kids lives? Simply by informing them to take the demon's advice that Satan is no angel of light. This is easy because, as you can imagine, these kids already know that catching hell is not fun.

This school year just came to an end and I am saddened, because helping these kids has exposed me to feelings I didn't know

I possessed.  However, the new school year is but a few months away. I proudly do what I do for the youths that are so easily overlooked; yet, I must admit that I constantly wonder about what could have been of my wretched life had somebody taken the time to give me some advice.  I once lived by the motto, "no regrets," but lately it's getting harder to relate to that phrase. But all things considered, I truly have no regrets when it comes to helping the children. My past may be a travesty, but their future doesn't have to be.

**Revision**  by Allington Dante Dottin


This Poem—is revision[1] . . .

---

[1] This is a one line poem. This Poem was conceived by a thought impregnated by Sha'condria ... This Poem demanded itself into being ... existed, and then ... insisted on being unlike any other This Poem poem ...

This Poem is not to bust shots or drip lust or lead ... Even though Its Author is, This Poem is not compelled to be hip-hop or like it must Dred ... Just like its Author, This Poem is Blood-Red ... Yet This Poem listens intently & seriously considers everything this Crip poem just said ...

This Poem recognizes that the true enemy doesn't live in rust red ... brick, dilapidated tenement houses in the slums ... but the white marble colonnaded ones ... that, with discrete precision, frames children for failure, imprisons, fathers in freeze frames, and this division, forces mothers to cross-dress (parentally speaking), in the absence of spouses ...

This Poem rhymes, but it doesn't have to ... This Poem has a choice ... like the option to sit in the front of the bus simply to pay tribute to Its Mothers' Mandated Manners, yes, the honor of relinquishing this convenient perch to an Elder Manuscript ... Or, a really pretty Poem ...

This Poem has the option to sit in the back, for observational purposes, daydreaming on that really pretty poem until those thoughts coalesce and conceive to pro-create little sticky pad poems ... that we hope will be raised into full white sheets ... But without the white sheet mentality ... Or the Black Hoodie fatality rate ...

This Poem gives good advice ... even though, that advice might make the poem It is advising even better than Itself ... This Poem gives away performance tips, techniques & tricks for when you get stuck, because ... well, who wants to win because the other poem got stuck?

This Poem wants to win the crown fair and diamond-esque ... even if it's only by point-fucking-one ... It wants to stand tall, pushing out its chest, for a full 31 seconds of glory, and THEN ... Be sincerely humble about it, for the rest of the entire year ...

This Poem overstands, that everything does not revolve around This Poem ... and when It does display that alarmingly human trait ... It gets over it. It overcomes its insatiable desire to always be center stage, thereby allowing someone else the spotlight for a minute ... or three ...

This Poem wishes slams could be judged & won based solely on crowd response, but only if they are all complete, absolute strangers to everyone here, and ... preferably in tears ...
This Poem lobbies for an emotional BS detector on stage, so when This Poem chokes up (as it invariably will), when ink runs freely from the three eyes adorning the right side of Its face, all would realize that it is not affectation ...

This Poem knows, intimately, why Its Author can never complete, from start to finish, the piece entitled, "Why I Write" ... not even in practice ... or in a workshop ... or in the shower ... In fact, This Poem wants the shower session all to Itself ...

This poem rails ... but now opts to offer solutions—or at least provoke and suggest thoughts of one— right alongside the issue being railed at ... Challenging? Yes ... But This Poem feels up to it ...

This poem is part of Exchange-for-Change ... and that means something ... It means

This Poem can be exactly how It is ... and that's okay ... But It better not stay that way ... I mean, It can be essentially the same poem, but the consciousness and/or compassion of the writing must continue to flow ... And it is virtually impossible for This Poem to cause Its Author to grow as a Writer, without growing, as a Person ...

This is a one line poem, with a really long footnote justifying why ... This Poem is Revision.

**Size 11, Baby Steps**  by Luis Hernandez

I was a normal healthy baby, that's what the doctor told my parents. As I got older they probably thought he lied to them. I can't remember my beginning. I have no knowledge of being in my mother's stomach. Or of seeing the light for the first time when I came out.  My parents heard my first cry, my first word—they saw my first steps. We were told some of these things. But who remembers the first time they did these things?  They told some us we were good babies; only a few were told they were little devils. They reminisced on all the fond memories they had of us. We know that we did these acts because we have seen other babies do them.  But we don't remember the experience. Some of us had credible witnesses; we don't doubt their word.

My first memories are vague. I remember a few. Crying, vomiting some pizza in a car, feeling hungry, being scared, and feeling happiness for a birthday—which one, I don't remember. The unforgettable first time I was suspended from school in kindergarten for having a pocket knife and some kid cut his hand. The feeling of fear and uncertainty afterwards. The indecision of putting my hand on a bubble gum pack for the first time and putting it in my pocket.  Looking at the rows of colorful candies, lusting so bad my eyes were on R.E.M overdrive. Why is it that the bad experiences are easy to remember?

Who hasn't struggled with identity crisis? We wanted to be super heroes. We wanted to be movie stars, to be somebody important; a person with meaning in life. Remember this question: "What do you want to be when you grow up?"

Nobody said a murderer, a thief, an infamous rapist, a bum, a drug addict, a male or female prostitute. Many live with the guilt of failure and in a perpetual identity crisis. Living a hopeless, defeated life. Contemplating suicide or embracing another person's lifestyle. Becoming a magician, wearing masks, disguising who we really are.

There is no denying we have been born once. What did we become? I became a follower of evil. If it was dangerous, harmful to my health, causing others pain, anger and suffering, that was my way of living. I could identify with a thief, a drug addict, a selfish piece of used flavorless chewing gum. My usefulness was like a bottomless garbage can. I wanted to be infamous. I thought that was a great aspiration. In my blindness, I saw nothing better. I wanted lots of stolen money, and fame for being an outstanding criminal. I couldn't go anywhere or do anything without getting high. I was sinking in my stupid ways, but I could not save myself.

I was also under pressure from friends—were they my friends? Have you been with people who caused you to decay and encouraged you to destroy your life? Turned your own family against you? But I had to live up to their expectations. I had to be what they idolized. I turned my back on my mother and father's example. They wanted me to work hard like they did and become an asset to society. An honest, respectful, good example of a immigrant who became someone successful in America. They tried, but they lost me, and I became the opposite. Their enemy.

Once you become a wild goat, can you go back to being a sheep? How could I break free from the chains that pulled me downward? I wanted no help; I didn't know I needed the evil gangrene to be cut off. It spread to the point where I was a hopeless criminal. I had to prove I was what I claimed to be, to myself and those who thought they knew me. They spoke highly of me. They said, "Luis will break into any house and rob anyone," and, "he is the one to be with on any robbery. The first one to break in with no hesitation." My reputation was important and I couldn't let them down. I thought it was what I was destined to be.

Have you ever felt like you were born to be something? I was stuck in a perpetual vicious cycle. Some days I hated myself. Why? I don't remember. I forgot what I wanted to be when I was a child, and I thought that desire died along with the past. It gets to the point where we become okay with what is despised. We act out and then embrace that identity that people give us. Maybe what our parents wanted or what our friends convicted us to be. Or we chose out of spite or rebellious pride. Something we never thought or dreamed of is what we became.

I definitely needed a new life. Have you ever thought about that? I didn't know it was available. I paid no attention to anything that could help me. I didn't care until I ruined myself and was in need of astronomical help. Facing a bottomless pit of time. I was kidnapped by the county jail. In need of saving, I thought, from 20 or 30 years in prison. The truth is that I needed saving from myself.

I had the knowledge and understanding of a thirteen year old, but I was eighteen. They did me a great favor. Have you ever hated people you thought ruined your life? To later find out that they actually helped you? What took my life away really gave me a new one. John 3:3 says, "Unless a grain of wheat gets buried and dies, it remains alone, but if it dies, it bears much fruit."

I prayed for help and got something unexpected, a new birth, spiritually. At first they were baby steps. I read a little bit of the Bible. I prayed and went to church. Like a newborn, there was thirst and hunger for the milk of the word. Things I never thought of or wanted to do . . . I started doing them. Attending church services, listening for an hour or two. I mean *paying attention*. Then my time spent reading increased. There was a desire to learn and hear worship and praise songs so I could sing them. Like learning a new language or speaking for the first time.

I grew and continue to develop my new identity. I believe in my first birth, but the second one—I personally *experienced* it. I remember my first spiritual steps and nobody had to tell me. I saw, and I continue to see growth in my life. The things I liked, I now hate: stealing, smoking, even lying.  The boring betterment, educational, Godly things: I now delight in them. Did I change? Am I a "new creature" like the bible says?  I cannot deny the meaning and purpose in my life now. I used to detest writing. I know this change is not only for me, it's available to others.  Those who want a new life and need a new birth.

What if I fall and go back to my old ways?  I don't worry about that, because I will continue to get back up and let the new man in me strive.

I was trash, discarded and put away to decay.  But, trash can be recycled and made new again. If they didn't tell us it was recycled, we wouldn't know.  I'm still getting processed, continually growing from the second birth. Who doesn't want to go from being nothing to becoming something great?  Who wouldn't go from being tossed in the dumpster to finding life in the recycling center?

**Remember, Wake Me When I Scream**  by Parnell Smith


You'll never recapture past days gone by.

Still you do your damnedest, they're memories trying

to hold on.

Birthdays and smiles of kids you don't know,

hoping someone captured them on their iPhone.


80's, 90's, deep after 2010's,

this generation, hears your name,

but only know of where you've been:

hidden away, deep inside the hall of shame.


Let me think,

how the hell did this happen to me?

I was raised with morals and principles.

Believing in Jesus Christ!

Was it somewhere along the road,

tricked, hoodwinked, bamboozled,

Elementary, Jr., or Sr., that my heart became ice?


*Song:*

> *I remember—Not too long ago—*

> *I went to a theatre—To see Kool + The Gang Show—*

*I've always wanted—yeah—to be the top man—*

*—oh-ooh-oh—*

*Stuck deep inside this prison, ya'll—With chains on feet +*
hands—

Whoa, whoa! Whoa! Whoa!!!

Not the song I remember.

Not the way life's supposed to go.

This has to be a bad dream, Lord,

this bed, feels like I'm sleeping on the flo'.

Roomy, hey brah,

You know what you've heard and seen,

don't let me go under, please.

Remember, *Wake Me When I Scream* . . .


*Wake Me When I Scream*

*Please, Somebody, Anybody,*

*Wake Me When I Scream,*

    *Heeeeeeeeeelp !?@* * . . .*

**Greater?** by Luis Aracena

"You and I are smart men, Luis, but I feel that we are not doing 'greater' things than we are capable of."

That's what a fellow inmate expressed to me after the 2016 Exchange for Change Winter Graduation. That statement created a desire to discover if indeed we are not doing greater things and, if not, what can we do to change that.

After long thought I concluded that we are, after all, doing greater things indeed. I remembered the graduation and saw how through Kathie and her awesome cast of volunteers, in a concerted effort with us convicts, are creating in the state of Florida an unprecedented awareness as to the capability and humanity of the wretched.

The graduation revealed the talents, skills and gifts of intellect and arts possessed by us, the wretched, that literally have the world raving and amazed at the level of brilliance found in prison, to the extent that lawmakers, judges, entertainers, professors, and other members of "polite" society cannot await the next opportunity to experience what can only be called "life changing." And without exaggeration, this description fails to convey the impact of the experience. As a result of this experience, I've seen all kinds of people start doing everything within their means to make the world aware of the forgotten treasures found in prison. This shows that we are using the vehicle provided by Exchange for Change to enlighten and educate the public, and at the same time introduce positive change into the penal system. Thus, I feel, think, and believe religiously that all of this, on its own merit, equates to, "doing something greater."

Nevertheless, what I find most rewarding about this program is the newfound respect and appreciation found amongst fellow prisoners, due to all the talent that is being showcased— something that would be impossible without educational opportunities. For instance, I used to view all other prisoners as a possible threat, a fear that is inbred through propaganda and stigmatization, but now I see them a potential pioneers in any and everything they so choose. I no longer see a danger but a person, highly capable and full of potential.

In light of all these facts, the overwhelming success this program has had, thus far, is but the tip of the iceberg: Yes we are doing greater things, yet what fills my heart with joy and abounding hope is the realization that even greater things are yet to come. I once heard, "If you wake up thought in a man, you could never put it to sleep," but now I know it, because I've experienced what this means. Truly we are on the path to greatness through awareness. The results speak for themselves, and Exchange for Change, alongside us convicts, has delivered time and again.

And if you did not know, you better ask somebody.  Or better yet, come and experience it for yourself.

**Parking Meters**  by Eduardo Martinez


Between sunflowers in the attic and bright

children in the basement,

     there is . . .



A politically-invested private parking lot with

     empty placements

Nothing vacant but fading signals of hope

     flickering red as . . . warnings

The mornings when

mo-NOT-ony

rocks our freedom to sleep

     our worlds are shaped

by a dividing line of secret segregation

     living in times

   where the yin-yang sign seems racist

   placed in isolated spaces

tattooed faces, with crooked grins, lit and set ablaze

   like Jack-o'-lanterns and just as


     H o l l o w

Baptized in the shallow waters of jury pools

burdens of forgotten friends bitten by the

    jagged fangs of a broken Heineken

    the melody of . . . sirens

    The night lights and lullaby of ghetto children

    . . .

    where sunrises die young,


    where you see the logic of Plan B, being A Plan, for an

unwanted seed . . .

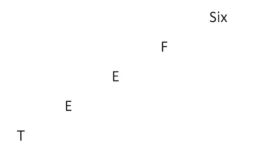

                     The Greed

                 Schemes

             Six

          F

       E

     E

  T

Deep dreams

that hang like Koala bears from a bubble-gum-popper's

bamboo earring like endangered species

child support

    or court hearings . . . proceeding,

to find a meaning between diapers and,


LIFERS


Both shitted on and discarded

The stigmata of a conscious convict

starving for a break from

DARKNESS

An escape from the mistake that roots for us,

as if it . . . grew us

Black      Brown      Tan

left Blue and bruised up

State raising juveniles to screw up . . .

It's Screw us . . .

It's screws loose


Choked by a profitable systematic noose


a concrete garden guarded by fresh-out-of-high-school flashlights

cops that hold the power of lightning bolts...

Uncle Sam's Frankenstein bolts . . .


Results of experimental Stanford Prison Projects

The contrast of cons ever getting accepted in college

The irrational rations of edible garbage

   for such grown men who swallow their pride daily like vitamins.

Satisfying their hunger with the


Snide                       Sneer                     Snicker


of an officer's anger, who is not yet old enough to rent a car

but old enough to confine a man old enough to be their Father

behind bars

     for simply being smarter


        Being sharper

             Going harder

                  Seducing karma

As we weld our scars into shields

'cause Band-Aids don't stick well on war fields

So what lies in here...

♥

               crumbles

GIANTS

or snaps mental midgets,


   PETA would have a fit if they put a poodle in this.

Is that proof that dogs are more important?

Or that we are non-existent?


Humans enslaved to bird cages covered by white sheets to
obscure society and keep us from talking
This is what makes men break . . . the wrong way often . . .
Accepting this cage like a single mother of five surviving in a one
bedroom section 8 estate
the fate of low income
the way the state,
Shakes

the

Spoon                                        on truthful food . . .


for thought
robbing us of . . .
Everything we never had the chance to love.
A sickness, that sits in us, like 49ers quarterback Kaepernick
as this country parades by us with floats of false hope,
'Til it's behind us.
Leaving us to chase the ghost of our past
like Pac-Man . . .


'Til we've eaten up our memories.
Spoon-shakers, starving us of a future

worth fighting for.

       Incarcerated    Inactivated    Activist

       Posted       or Decades

       In 8x10 parking spots

       Soldiers

       Sentinels

       Generals

       Pawns

       Cemented in cinder blocks

       Prisoners

         Awaiting

            Silently

Demanding change, but doing nothing

. . . like parking meters.

Exchange for Change provides opportunities for creative and intellectual engagement.

We believe in the value of every voice, and we give our students an opportunity to express themselves without the fear of being stigmatized. When everyone has the ability to listen and be heard, strong and safe communities are formed.

Collaboration is our emphasis. Students on the outside anonymously partner with imprisoned writers to foster empathy and create opportunities for individual and social change, allowing both sides to learn from the knowledge and experiences of their writing partners, all while realizing the value of events in their own lives.

With a pen and paper, students can become agents of change across different communities in ways they may otherwise have never encountered.

## OUR MISSION

The nonprofit Exchange for Change teaches writing in prisons and runs letter exchanges between incarcerated students and writers studying on the outside. By preparing prisoners for their reentry into the outside community and preparing that community for their return, Exchange for Change provides vision and understanding on both sides of the fence.

.

## ADVISORY BOARD

Russell Banks

Reginald Dwayne Betts

Marcelyn Cox

Edwidge Danticat

Mitchell Kaplan

Claudia Kitchens

Elizabeth Barash Murphy

Leonard Pitts, Jr.

## TEAM

Phillip Agnew

Jill Berke

Farris Bukhari

Enzu Castellanos

Jacqueline Coleman

Maria Cristina Fernandez

George Franklin

Malcolm Jackson

Meena Jagannath

Ken Johnson

Sara Kedan

Maya Keiffer

Qamara Kurtz

Allison Langer

Benjamin Moats

Aja Monet

Yaddyra Peralta

Henry Unger

Nick Vagnoni

Carlos Velazco

## PARTNERS

Dade Youth Academy

Emory University

Florida Atlantic University

Florida International University

Florida Department of Corrections

Florida Department of Juvenile Justice

Miami Dade College

Miami Youth Academy

O, Miami

Ransom Everglades School

University of Miami

To discuss underwriting opportunities, for additional copies of this journal, subscriptions, or to help and/or participate, contact Exchange for Change at:

**www.exchange-for-change.org**